W9-AVL-788

ISBN 0 86112 637 8
© Brimax Books Ltd 1990. All rights reserved.
Published by Brimax Books Ltd, Newmarket, England 1990.
Printed in Hong Kong.

Riddles · and · Rhymes

by Elizabeth Fletcher
Illustrated by Dorothea King

Brimax Books • Newmarket • England

Riddles and Rhymes is a fun way of presenting questions and answers. The question is in the form of an easy-to-read riddle. Each riddle is surrounded by picture clues which help the child find the answer. By simply turning the page, the child will find the fully illustrated answer. To find out if they are correct, children can turn to the back of the book for written answers.

I like to pay a visit
About this time of year,
And you are glad to see me
When I suddenly appear;
For if it's very cold
You can play with me all day
But when the sun shines brightly,
Quickly I'll go away.

What am I?

Look at me and you will find
A trumpet of a different kind,
I'm very pretty too I'm told,
I'm found in shops where I am sold;
On me a tune you cannot play,
When spring is gone, I fade away.

What am I?

A button-shaped nose
And two tufted ears,
I live far away
Across the sea;
I look like a bear
But live among leaves
Of the eucalyptus tree.

What am I?

I dream of open spaces,
A real flowing mane,
A fast exciting gallop
Across a sandy plain;
But as you climb upon me
And laugh contentedly,
You know I cannot ride away
And then I'm glad I'm me.

What am I?

You'll find I'm very bright
And pretty too, they say,
But you cannot see me
Until dark clouds roll away,
And then I shall appear
When the sun peeps through again,
A bow to brighten up your day
As sunshine follows rain.

What am I?

Although I am not real
You like my company
And sometimes I am shabby
But you still care for me;
I am never far away
If you need me day or night,
And when you're very sleepy
You just cuddle me up tight.

What am I?

I am found in parks
Or playgrounds close to you,
Where you like to play
With friends the whole day through;
If you go up you must come down
By now you will have found,
And once again you'll laugh and climb
When you reach the ground

What am I?

I rise up every morning,
I'm never up at night,
Children love to see me
When I am warm and bright;
But if I'm hot and strong
Each flower drops its head,
And gardeners complain
And wish for rain instead.

                               What am I?

When children hang their stockings
At the bottom of the bed,
I'm bought in shops and markets,
I'm prickly, green and red.

What am I?

No fingers, one thumb,
But easy they say,
For children to wear
On a cold, windy day.

What am I?

As my sails go round
The corn is ground,
In country places
I am found.

What am I?

I run very fast,
My legs are long,
When others are tired
I am still going strong;
My head is quite small,
My neck is stretched high,
I am the largest bird
But I cannot fly.

                    What am I?

I stretch as far as you can see,
Sometimes I'm out when you want me;
I'm in and out every day,
And when I'm in you'll laugh and play.

What am I?

Look closely and you will find
A home of a different kind,
For I'm not built with stones or bricks
But moss, leaves and broken sticks;
I'm found near banks, hedgerows too,
Or hidden high away from you.

What am I?

Special time,
Special name,
Different sizes,
Shape's the same;
Some we keep
To eat that day,
Some we buy
To give away.

What are we?

I have a bushy tail
And bright, brown eyes,
My home is in a tree
I've built up high;
I am never hungry
When snow is on the ground,
Before summer ends
My food I'll have found.

What am I?

You'll find me in the morning
And also late at night,
You need warm clothes when I'm about
So wrap up snug and tight;
I make patterns on your window,
I turn the grass white, too,
Now read the first two lines again
And then then you'll have a clue.

                    What am I?

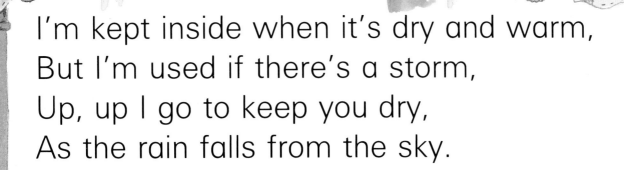

I'm kept inside when it's dry and warm,
But I'm used if there's a storm,
Up, up I go to keep you dry,
As the rain falls from the sky.

What am I?

I nibble green lettuce
To make me grow strong,
My tail's soft and fluffy,
But not very long;
My ears listen out
As I race with ease,
Then rest in the cornfield,
Or play in the breeze.

What am I?

I'm very pretty when I'm lit
For everyone to see,
But suddenly my lights go out
And that's the end of me;
I'm cut then eaten as they sing
A happy birthday cheer,
And no one misses me
As I quickly disappear.

What am I?

You build me up to knock me down
Far away from shops and town;
I'm found near sea, both wet and dry,
With a flag flying high.

What am I?

Branches that shimmer,
One fairy dressed in white,
Hanging decorations,
A twinkling star so bright,
Make believe snow
And tinsel here and there,
Gifts tied with bows,
You decorate me each year.
                    What am I?

If I give a little clue
You'll soon see what I mean,
Because my legs are long and thin,
Only one is often seen.

What am I?

Grown in orchards, gardens too,
People say I'm good for you;
Red or yellow, sometimes green,
In shops and markets I am seen.
What am I?

I'm used at night,
Made up all day,
I have four legs
But cannot play;
I'm made with sheets
And pillows too,
On me you sleep
The whole night through.

What am I?

55

I cannot fly, I cannot run,
I shelter from the mid-day sun,
Upon my back my house is placed,
I crawl along, but once I raced;
And now when danger lurks around,
Inside I pop, all safe and sound.

What am I?

If you look inside me
My face you cannot see,
For as you look through me,
Another face there'll be;
They call it a reflection,
Of your face, not mine
And as you move away
I will gleam and shine.

What am I?

First I grew a tail,
Then my legs appeared,
I grew a little bigger
And my tail disappeared;
I'm very good at swimming,
I can hop high off the ground,
And you will know I'm near,
When you hear a croaking sound!

What am I?

You kick me here, you kick me there,
You throw me high into the air;
You can bounce me all around
Or roll me gently on the ground.

What am I?

Beaten well, then tossed up high,
Made on a special date;
But as I am so tasty,
Sometimes you cannot wait.

What am I?

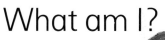

The name of my nose
Is part of a tree,
And I use it
When you feed me;
My skin's very tough
All wrinkled and grey,
I'm often found
In zoos today.

                    What am I?

I wear a little collar
And on it is my name,
My lead is held firmly
When walking down the lane;
My tail is long and furry,
My nose is wet and cold,
I'm sometimes found in pet shops
Where I am often sold.

What am I?

I'm not very pretty
When you look at me,
But one day I'll change,
Just wait and see.
Instead of eating leaves
As birds loudly sing,
I'll fly on the breeze
With graceful wings.

What am I?

Black and white
Slowly I run,
But children find
I'm full of fun;
I'm not a duck
But I waddle too,
I'm often found
Inside a zoo.

What am I?

I squeal very loud
As I wander about,
I slide in the mud
And dig with my snout;
My tail curls up tightly,
I live in a sty,
When I'm cold and hungry
I will cry.

What am I?

I'm playful and young,
I lap with my tongue,
Curled on the rug,
Cosy and snug;
When I'm happy I purr,
I'm a small ball of fur.

What am I?

People sail upon me
As I flow to the sea,
I'm sometimes very gentle
But can flow stormily;
In places I am narrow
But in others very wide,
You can fish from my shore
And picnic by my side.

What am I?

My father's a ram,
My mother's a ewe,
My coat's warm and thick,
I'm woolly and new.

What am I?

I'm always very playful
With four, soft paws,
If teased or angry
I scratch with my claws;
My mother's roar
Is loud and strong,
She roams the plains,
Where we belong.

                What am I?

84

I have two handles and a wheel
By now you will have found,
I can help you carry loads,
You push me all around.

What am I?

In summer I'm busy as can be,
But winter time you'll not see me;
I stay at home until next spring
When flowers bloom and cuckoos sing.

What am I?

With fire in my tail
And my nose pointing high,
I'm off to the moon
As I speed through the sky.

What am I?

I live deep in the jungle
And walk on four, soft paws,
I am the biggest of all cats
And if you're near . . . I'll roar!

What am I?

I travel far on windy days,
When boys and girls are out to play,
Then higher and higher they watch me fly,
They tug the string, I reach the sky.

What am I?

I gallop fast with flowing mane
Along the quiet country lane;
When I'm hungry, I will neigh
Until the farmer feeds me hay.

What am I?

We sparkle in the dark night sky,
Whizzing as we shoot up high;
Pink, yellow, blue and green,
For miles around we can be seen;
And on a very special date
We can help you celebrate!

What are we?

Riding on the ferris wheel
Can be a lot of fun,
Or buying red balloons
That shine in the sun;
Children laugh and shout
On the merry-go-round,
Where they are having fun
You know I can be found.

What am I?

Placed on a shelf or on the wall,
I have two hands, one big, one small;
I have a face, no nose or lips,
The noise inside me tick-tock-ticks.

What am I?

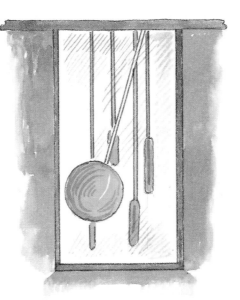

When I am frozen hard
It's safe to skate on me,
And children laugh and shout
As they play happily,
But please don't skate upon me
When I am cracked and thin,
For then I'm very dangerous;
Keep off or you'll fall in.

What am I?

Just a small speck
As I soar through the sky,
Strange roaring noises
As upwards I fly;
Crossing the ocean,
Then home safe and sound,
My wings will glisten
As I land on the ground.

What am I?

People like to eat us
For we are good for you,
And sometimes if you're thirsty
You can drink us too;
One of us is yellow
But the other cannot say,
For if we were to tell you
We would give the game away.

What are we?

I really come from Africa,
But can be seen in zoos,
I look like a horse
And a donkey too;
You really can't mistake me,
I am a funny sight,
I'm sure you will know
My black and white stripes.

What am I?

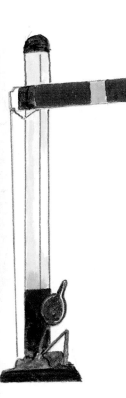

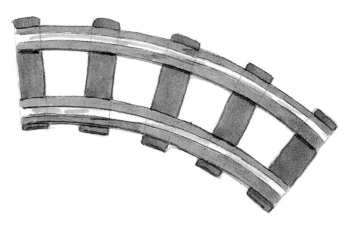

People travel in me
As I speed along the track,
I take them on their journey
And then I bring them back,
I cannot race along a road
Or fly high in the sky,
But if you hear a chuffing noise,
You'll know I'll soon pass by.

What am I?

112

I've just arrived, I've come to town,
The children love the red-nosed clown,
He makes them laugh and shout with glee,
As horses curtsy on their knees.
The lions roar, trick after trick,
The trainer cracks his leather whip.
The dogs jump high, dance on their toes
For people sitting, row by row;
The children are tired, it's been such fun,
Now home to bed, the day is done.

What am I?

Hold me tight
And I'll hold you,
Balancing together,
Away we go.

What am I?

I hunt in woods and gardens
With black, beady eyes,
My young are hatched in nests,
Some say I'm very wise;
My beak is hooked, my claws are strong,
I sleep throughout the day,
With feathers that are soft and smooth
Quietly, I fly away.

What am I?

ANSWERS

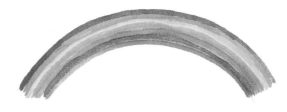

15 Rainbow

7 Snow

17 Teddy bear

9 Daffodil

19 Slide

11 Koala

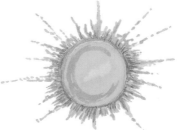

21 The sun

13 Rocking horse

23 Holly

120

25 Mitten

27 Windmill

29 Ostrich

31 The sea

33 Nest

35 Easter eggs

37 Squirrel

39 Frost

41 Umbrella

43 Rabbit

45 Birthday cake

47 Sandcastle

49 Christmas tree

51 Flamingo

53 Apple

55 Bed

57 Tortoise

59 Mirror

61 Frog

63 Ball

65 Pancake

75 Piglet

67 Elephant

77 Kitten

69 Puppy

79 River

71 Caterpillar

81 Lamb

73 Penguin

83 Lion cub

85 Wheelbarrow

95 Horse

87 Bee

97 Fireworks

89 Rocket

99 Fair

91 Tiger

101 Clock

93 Kite

103 Frozen pond

105 Plane

107 Oranges and lemons

109 Zebra

111 Train

113 Circus

115 Bike

117 Owl